ALSO BY PEARL CLEAGE

NOVELS

Babylon Sisters
Some Things I Never Thought I'd Do
I Wish I Had a Red Dress
What Looks Like Crazy on an Ordinary Day . . .

NONFICTION

Mad at Miles: A Black Woman's Guide to Truth
Deals with the Devil and Other Reasons to Riot

We Speak Your Names

ONE WORLD
BALLANTINE BOOKS
NEW YORK

We Speak Your Names

A CELEBRATION

PEARL CLEAGE

with Zaron W. Burnett, Jr.

Published in the United States by One World Books,
an imprint of The Random House Publishing Group,
a division of Random House, Inc., New York.
A portion of this title was published
in the August 2005 issue
of *O Magazine*.

ONE WORLD is a registered trademark and the One World
colophon is a trademark of Random House, Inc.

Library of Congress Cataloging-in-Publication Data

Cleage, Pearl.
We speak your names : a celebration / Pearl Cleage with
Zaron W. Burnett, Jr.
p.   cm.
ISBN 0-345-49027-4
1. African American women—Poetry.   I. Burnett, Zaron W.   II. Title.
PS3553.L389W425 2005
811'.54—dc22   2005051826

Printed on acid-free paper in the United States of America

www.oneworldbooks.net

246897531

FIRST EDITION

Book design by Carole Lowenstein

To Mrs. Johnsie Broadway Burnett

Contents

Introduction

xi

We Speak Your Names: A Celebration

1

The Legends

17

Introduction

On February 21, 2005, I received an invitation from Oprah Winfrey to write a piece for what she was calling her *Legends Weekend.* The occasion had taken shape in her mind almost a year before, beginning life as a small luncheon and evolving into a three-day event honoring twenty-five legendary African American women whose lives and careers are what people mean when they use the term "role model." She was also inviting forty-two other women, whom she was calling the "young 'uns" and who would share with her this unique opportunity to celebrate this amazing group. To my surprise and great delight, not only had I been included among the "young 'uns" (my two beautiful grandchildren notwithstanding!), I was now being asked to write a piece that would express our collective thank-you to our symbolic foremothers. I said I would be honored, so she sent me the names of the legends and the young 'uns and left me to my own devices.

Looking at the list, I immediately realized I didn't need to collect biographical information about these women. You could wake me up from a sound sleep in the middle of the night, and I could tell you not only who they are but who they are *to me.* Oprah's list of honorees mirrored my own personal most–admired list, from Maya Angelou to Nancy Wilson, and just reading their names stirred up a lifetime's worth of memories. I had danced to their music, been inspired by their courage, envied the artful arrangement of their words on paper, and torn their pictures out of magazines to post where I could see them, bold and beautiful, as they redefined style and substance and sisterhood.

So I did what I always do: I started making notes. Enlisting the assistance of my husband, Zaron, I allowed the memories to come tumbling out in no particular order. By the time we returned home to Atlanta after a two–week road trip (we don't like to fly!), we had more than enough material, and I had enough sense to know that the piece was evolving into something more than a poem. It was becoming the sisterhood ritual we needed. I wrote it in one long *whoosh* and sent it by overnight mail to

Miz Oprah, who liked it as much as I did. My part was done. All I had to do now was find a ball gown I wouldn't trip over, pick up our train tickets to Santa Barbara, and get back to work on my novel. A month went by, and then suddenly it was time to go to California.

The weekend, which was now officially known as *A Bridge to Now: A Celebration of Remarkable Women in Remarkable Times,* began with a luncheon at Oprah's home, to which only the legends and the young 'uns were invited. No dates, no spouses, no anxious publicists or protective mamas. It was just us, and somehow in the absence of other people we became simply a room full of free women, celebrating one another and ourselves and our sisterhood. The poem was read for the first time at that luncheon. That's where it came to life in a small gazebo where we gathered to sing our praise song.

Speaking on behalf of the young 'uns, I joined Angela Bassett and Alfre Woodard and Phylicia Rashad and Halle Berry in paying tribute to our legends. Beside us stood six of the *younger* young 'uns— Mariah Carey, Janet Jackson, Alicia Keys, Ashanti, Mary J. Blige, and Missy Elliott—in a chorus that led us in the refrain: *We speak your names. We speak your names.* And all around us were our sisters in the flesh, weeping and laughing and hugging one another in recognition of how amazing they truly are, and our sisters in the spirit, gone but never forgotten, celebrating with us and forgiving us completely for taking so long to call them back and tell them *thank you.* It was a moment when no one could deny the magic or describe it, so we didn't try.

The next night, we added the other young 'uns—Yolanda Adams, Debbie Allen, Tyra Banks, Kathleen Battle, Naomi Campbell, Natalie Cole, Suzanne de Passe, Kimberly Elise, Pam Grier, Iman, Judith Jamison, Beverly Johnson, Chaka Khan, Gayle King, Darnell Martin, Terry McMillan, Audra McDonald, Melba Moore, Brandy Norwood, Michelle Obama, Suzan-Lori Parks, Valerie Simpson, Anna Deavere Smith, and Susan L. Taylor—to our chorus. At the glittering Legends Ball, we offered the poem one more time as a parting gift before we all headed home the next day to our busy, separate lives, promising not to forget what had happened among us, promising to stay in touch. And then it was over.

Three days after I stood in Oprah's garden, surrounded by a feeling of connectedness not only to the women whose names we had called but to the ones whose spirits we had raised whose names we never knew and never will, Zaron and I were driving home to Atlanta on Route 66. When we stopped for the night, I turned on the television, and suddenly, *there we were,* Oprah's Legends Ball, live and in living color, as the lead story on *Entertainment Tonight.* It startled me, not so much because I hadn't expected to see the event covered by the media, but because the story that I saw didn't get to the heart of the matter. *Yes,* there were stars. *Yes,* there were wonderful flowers, and fabulous gowns, and diamond earrings, and designer shoes, and caviar in silver spoons. The camera captured all of that perfectly. The only thing it missed was the presence of all those spirits who hadn't gone anywhere after that luncheon except right back to the ball with us, so that when we sang "Ain't No Mountain High Enough," they sang it, too. When we danced all night, *just because we could,* they were dancing, too. Which is the reason we are all smiling when you see us in those pictures. Because we do love our earrings, but in that one amazing moment, *we loved one another more, and more, and more, and more. . . .*

Being a worrier by nature, I turned off the television and immediately began to wonder how long it would be before the real feeling faded. I wondered how long before I could only remember *what happened*—who wore what and who sat where—but not *what it felt like to be there.* How long before it be-came a wonderful memory and nothing more. But we continued our journey home, and gradually the beauty of the landscape cleared my head, and the sweetness of the people we encountered soothed my soul, and at some point—I think it was when we stopped for the night outside of Amarillo, Texas—I stopped worrying. In that blessed moment of calm, I read the poem to myself out loud, and the feeling from the gazebo came back strong. The more I read, the less I worried about what I might forget and the more I understood that this was something I would always remember.

Oprah calls it a praise poem. I call it a celebra-tion for the same reason, because this piece is part of an oral tradition that goes back as far as we do: a tradition that grows out of an understanding that some things must be spoken out loud to get to where the magic is. *This poem is like that.* If it were a spell, I'd encourage you to cast it. Sisterhood in the service of truth is an undeniable force in these re-markable times. My Sisters, *here, there, and everywhere,* this poem is for you. *Use it, adapt it, pass it on. . . .*

We Speak Your Names:
A Celebration

Because we are free women,
born of free women,
who are born of free women,
back as far as time begins,
we celebrate your freedom.

Because we are wise women,
born of wise women,
who are born of wise women,
we celebrate your wisdom.

Because we are strong women,
born of strong women,
who are born of strong women,
we celebrate your strength.

Because we are magical women,
born of magical women,

who are born of magical women,
we celebrate your magic.

My sisters, we are gathered here to speak your
    names.
We are here because we are your daughters
as surely as if you had conceived us, nurtured us,
carried us in your wombs, and then sent us out
    into the world to make our mark
and see what we see, *and be what we be,* but *better,
    truer, deeper*
because of the shining example of your own
    incandescent lives.

We are here to speak your names
because we have enough sense to know
that we did not spring full blown from the
    forehead of Zeus,
or arrive on the scene like Topsy, our sister once
    removed, who somehow *just growed.*
We know that we are walking in footprints made
    deep by the confident strides
of women who parted the air before them like the
    forces of nature that you are.

We are here to speak your names

because you taught us that the search is always for
    the truth
and that when people show us who they are, we
    should believe them.

We are here because you taught us
that *sisterspeak* can continue to be our native
    tongue,
no matter how many languages we learn as we
    move about as citizens of the world
and of the ever-evolving universe.

We are here to speak your names
because of the way you made for us.
Because of the prayers you prayed for us.
We are the ones you conjured up, hoping we
    would have strength enough,
and discipline enough, and talent enough, and
    nerve enough
to step into the light when it turned in our
    direction, *and just smile awhile.*

We are the ones you hoped would make you
    proud
because all of our hard work

makes all of yours part of something *better, truer, deeper.*

Something that lights the way ahead like a lamp unto our feet,

as steady as the unforgettable beat of our collective heart.

We speak your names.
We speak your names.

DR. MAYA ANGELOU
SHIRLEY CAESAR
DIAHANN CARROLL
ELIZABETH CATLETT
RUBY DEE
KATHERINE DUNHAM

We speak your names.
We speak your names.

You could not have known how closely we watched your every move.

How we hung on your every word.

How eagerly we ran to sit cross-legged in front of the television

whenever you were on *Ed Sullivan* or *Soul Train*
or *60 Minutes.*

How patiently we saved our money to buy that
record, or that theatre ticket,
or that museum membership, or that magazine
subscription
that would allow us to see you doing what nobody
else had ever done before,
in just that way, on every front, *all at the same time.*

We were so proud of you, it made us walk taller,
smile wider, dream bigger.

You could not have been in each of our little black
girl bedrooms,
watching us hold that *make-pretend* microphone
as we lip–synched your latest hit when dinner was
ready downstairs,
or curled up under the covers with your new book
when we had math homework to do,
or prayed for your safety when our parents told us
you were somewhere
fighting for our freedom, and it was dangerous
work.

It is always dangerous work, but the trade-off is
    unacceptable.
From you we learned that freedom is
    non-negotiable.

You could not have known that your collective
    example
of the limitless possibilities that were open to us
is what allowed us to look our mothers in the eye
    and say:
Mama, I want to be a singer.
Mama, I want to be an actress.
Mama, I want to be a dancer, or a sculptor, or a
    lawyer, or a leader,
Or a world-changing force for good, loose in the
    world, *and whirling.* . . .

And even when she rolled her eyes and shook her
    head
and pronounced us more our father's child than
    we had ever been hers,
she knew *you* had planted those ideas in our heads,
and she thanked you for letting us see
that we could be a part of something *better, truer,*
    deeper.

We speak your names.
We speak your names.

ROBERTA FLACK
ARETHA FRANKLIN
NIKKI GIOVANNI
DR. DOROTHY HEIGHT
LENA HORNE
CORETTA SCOTT KING

We speak your names.
We speak your names.

Because we are sensual women,
born of sensual women,
who are born of sensual women,
we celebrate your passion.

You taught us that the mysteries of true love
are sometimes harder to unravel
than all the others we attempt to understand,
but that when we are lucky enough to find that
    thread,
the rewards are worth everything,
because the time to have enough of love is never.

Because we have had our hearts broken, we know
   your tears
and have felt the same fears of never finding one
   who can share our light
without getting lost in it, or tossed in it,
into a wind that always blows colder than we
   think it will.

We celebrate your willingness to continue to search
   for love,
and find it, and lose it, and find it, and lose it
   again
until we finally find it *for real*
and learn to hold on tight by not holding on at all.

From you, we learned that love, like beauty, comes
   in many forms.
You showed us what love looks like when it's
   perfect, and when it isn't.
You let us watch you looking, reaching, yearning,
always moving toward the light of something
   better, truer, deeper.

We speak your names.
We speak your names.

Gladys Knight
Patti LaBelle
Dr. Toni Morrison
Rosa Parks
Leontyne Price
Della Reese
Diana Ross

We speak your names.
We speak your names.

And you made it look so easy.

You change the world around you with such fierce
    determination,
effortless style, and unshakeable grace
that we never suspected how hard it was to be out
    there in the real world,
where sisterhood sometimes seems an abstract idea
and not the living, breathing thing we know and
    need and want it to be.

We have sometimes shivered at the edges of a very
    cold place,
where people do not always see our beauty
or understand the rhythm of our song.

At those moments, we whisper your names as a
    talisman and a touchstone,
so we will not forget who and what and why we
    are here.

And then, *sometimes*, in recognition of our superior
    skill, or our undeniable talent,
or our absolute refusal to bend in the face of
    injustice,
sometimes, we win the prize. *The big one.*
The one they will mention forever after when they
    call our names,
or write our reviews, or compose our obituaries.

Sometimes, at that crucial, *first one ever* moment,
we are invited to come to center court at
    Wimbledon,
or up to the Oscar podium, or the Oval Office, or
    the Nobel ceremony,
or the Broadway stage, and express our feelings
and the feelings of every other African American
    woman watching
at a moment when all we really want to do is call
    your names.

All we really want to do is thank all of you for
     being with all of us,
whenever and wherever we find ourselves,
     standing alone in the light.
At those moments, we remember those lessons you
     shared
by living your very public lives with such integrity
     and honor
that they became something *better, truer, deeper.*

We speak your names.
We speak your names.

NAOMI SIMS
TINA TURNER
CICELY TYSON
ALICE WALKER
DIONNE WARWICK
NANCY WILSON
OPRAH WINFREY

We speak your names.
We speak your names.

Because we are free women,
born of free women,

who are born of free women,
back as far as time begins,
we celebrate your freedom.

Because we are wise women,
born of wise women,
who are born of wise women,
we celebrate your wisdom.

Because we are magical women,
born of magical women,
who are born of magical women,
we celebrate your magic.

We celebrate your courage.
We celebrate your spirit.
We celebrate your genius.
We celebrate your lovingkindness.
We celebrate your faith in yourselves, and in us.

We thank you for the dues you've paid,
and the prayers you've prayed.

We thank you for showing us how to fly *by flying.*

We thank you for these wings,

and we stand before you now, *your living legacy,*
the flesh and blood of our collective dreaming,
and we realize with a knowing deeper than the
    flow of human blood in human veins
that we are part of something *better, truer, deeper.*

We speak your names.
We speak your names.

The Legends

Dr. Maya Angelou

Born April 4, 1928, St. Louis, Missouri;
bestselling author, poet, playwright, actress, stage
and screen producer, civil rights activist

My first memory of Maya Angelou is reading a copy of *I Know Why the Caged Bird Sings* and being overwhelmed by its courageous combination of truth, love, humor, and heartache. Watching her recite her poem "On the Pulse of the Morning" at the inauguration of President Clinton, I couldn't have been prouder to be a part of the sisterhood of black women writers as one of our own spoke for all Americans. She is a writer who always makes me want to work harder to *tell the story straight.*

SHIRLEY CAESAR
Born October 13, 1938, Durham, North Carolina;
gospel singer, minister, Broadway performer, eleven-time
Grammy winner, "First Lady of Gospel"

I defy you to listen to Shirley Caesar's classic gospel album *Stranger on the Road* and not find yourself filled with whatever spirit you believe in. That album helped me survive my thirties without losing perspective or hope. I still play "Loose That Man" every couple of Sundays, as loud as I think my neighbors can stand it. So far, I haven't had any complaints.

DIAHANN CARROLL
Born July 17, 1935, Bronx, New York;
Oscar- and Emmy-nominated film, television, and
Broadway actress; women's health activist

Every African American woman of a certain age re-
members when *Julia* debuted on television in 1968,
and I am no different. Diahann Carroll's presence on
that show broke down racial boundaries and gave
the African American community a chance to share
her talent, beauty, and grace with the world. But
it was the complexity and compassion that she
showed as the title character in the film *Claudine*,
playing against type as a struggling single mother,
that moved me more and earned her an Oscar nomi-
nation.

ELIZABETH CATLETT
Born April 15, 1915, Washington, D.C.;
sculptor, printmaker, activist

Truly a citizen of the world, Elizabeth Catlett creates work that is deeply rooted in and reflective of the African American experience without ever sacrificing the specificity of her unique artistic vision. Touching one of her exquisite sculptures is like connecting to the soul of a people and the heart of a woman.

RUBY DEE

Born October 27, 1924, Cleveland, Ohio;
stage, film, and television actress; frequent collaborator
with her husband, the late Ossie Davis, recipient of the
National Medal of the Arts and Kennedy Center Honors

I met Ruby Dee as a starstruck teenager when my father, a friend of Dee and Davis, took me backstage after her performance as Cassandra in the classic Greek drama *Agamemnon*. Both lifelong activists, they chatted about the state of the Movement, but I was in awe of her skill as an actress. More than thirty years later, it was an honor to have her play a lead role in my play *Flyin' West* at the Kennedy Center and to call her and Ossie my friends.

Katherine Dunham
Born June 22, 1909, Joliet, Illinois;
choreographer, dancer, founder of the Katherine Dunham
Dance Company, anthropologist, world traveler, teacher,
named among First 100 of America's Irreplaceable Dance
Treasures by the Dance Heritage Coalition

Incorporating elements of African, Caribbean, South African, and other ethnic styles into her dances, Katherine Dunham created a unique choreographic vocabulary. Her "Stormy Weather" ballet is a highlight of the classic film of the same name, which also features Lena Horne, William "Bojangles" Robinson, Cab Calloway, and the Nicholas Brothers.

ROBERTA FLACK
Born February 10, 1939, Asheville, North Carolina;
singer, songwriter, winner of multiple Grammy awards

When Roberta Flack's debut album, *First Take*, appeared in 1969, it was impossible not to hear "The First Time Ever I Saw Your Face" on everybody's radio or record player, and impossible not to be moved by it each time. We all wanted to be in love like that. Her duets with the late Donny Hathaway are still classics.

ARETHA FRANKLIN

Born March 25, 1942, Memphis, Tennessee;
singer, songwriter, pianist, winner of sixteen Grammy
awards, first woman inducted into the Rock and Roll
Hall of Fame, "Queen of Soul"

When I was growing up in Detroit, Rev. C. L. Franklin, Aretha's charismatic father, had a huge church a few blocks from my father's more radical, and considerably smaller, congregation. As we passed the crowd streaming into Rev. Franklin's church on Sunday morning my father would tease me that if I could sing like Aretha, our church would be standing room only, too. As much as I wanted to please him, I knew there was no chance of that happening. Nobody will ever sing like Aretha.

Nikki Giovanni
Born June 7, 1943, Knoxville, Tennessee;
poet, activist, teacher

I first met Nikki Giovanni when she was a girl poet from Cincinnati doing a reading at my father's church. She was an unapologetically female voice in a sea of macho male poets, carrying her books in the trunk of a beat-up old car, a perfect Afro crowning her head, and a smile on her face that said there was no better way to live if you were a woman in love with words and revolution—not necessarily in that order. She was right, too.

Dr. Dorothy Height

Born March 24, 1912, Richmond, Virginia;
activist, advocate, president of the National Council
of Negro Women from 1957 to 1998, recipient
of the Presidential Medal of Freedom

Dr. Height likes to tell a story of a lost election in Mississippi when the right to vote was still a life-and-death decision for many black Americans. She was angry that poor black sharecroppers had voted against their own interests to elect a white supremacist candidate who had promised them canned goods. Her friend and sister activist Fannie Lou Hamer shushed her with these simple words: *Those people aren't dumb. They're hungry.* It was a lesson she never forgot.

LENA HORNE

Born June 30, 1917, Brooklyn, New York;
dancer, film actress, singer, Broadway performer, recipient of
Kennedy Center Honors for lifetime contribution to the arts
and a Lifetime Achievement Grammy Award

I grew up listening to my father and my uncles extol the beauty of Lena Horne, but it wasn't until I had a chance to watch her in the 1943 film *Stormy Weather* that I understood she wasn't just beautiful. She was *everything*. Her performance of the movie's title song is a highlight. In 1981, when I saw her one–woman show, *Lena Horne: The Lady and Her Music,* her talent, beauty, and charisma were undiminished.

Coretta Scott King
Born April 27, 1927, Marion, Alabama;
musician, activist, author

My first job when I moved to Atlanta in 1969 was as a transcriber for the Martin Luther King, Jr., Library Documentation Project. In the midst of her grief, Mrs. King had already put together the beginnings of what would later become the Martin Luther King, Jr., Center for Nonviolent Social Change. That year, I spent my days with the voices of the Civil Rights Movement in my ears, grateful for a chance to be a part of the work Dr. King had left in his wife's capable hands.

GLADYS KNIGHT

Born May 28, 1944, Atlanta, Georgia;
singer, author, Grammy Award winner, inducted into the
Rock and Roll Hall of Fame in 1996, Lifetime Achievement
Award from the Rhythm and Blues Foundation in 1998

When I was living in Atlanta in the eighties, Gladys Knight sightings were not unusual, but always a treat. I remember once seeing her dining with friends in a small restaurant. As she got up to leave every head in the place turned to watch. Seeming to share our pleasure in her presence, she flashed us all her megawatt smile, slipped her black mink coat over her shoulders, and swept out, leaving behind the smell of her perfume and the unmistakable glitter of stardust.

Patti LaBelle

Born May 24, 1944, Philadelphia, Pennsylvania;
singer, Grammy Award winner, health activist, author

During a dynamic live performance when "Lady Marmalade" was the number one record in the country, Patti LaBelle had herself lowered onto the stage of the Atlanta Civic Center in an explosion of sequins and feathers like a beautiful bird who had just flown in from another galaxy. Those of us lucky enough to be in attendance screamed so loud and long that by the middle of the show, none of us had any voice left. But Patti did.

DR. TONI MORRISON

Born February 18, 1931, Lorain, Ohio;
author, editor, teacher, recipient of the National Book Award
in 1977, a Pulitzer Prize in 1988, and the Nobel Prize
for Literature in 1993

I was already in awe of *The Bluest Eye* when my friend and sister writer Toni Cade Bambara brought Toni Morrison over to my house for dinner. I was so terrified of burning the roast chicken or scorching the bottom of the cornbread that my only memory of the evening is asking her to sign my copy of her novel, and enjoying her pleasure in the French vanilla ice cream we had for dessert. I still have the book.

Rosa Parks

Born February 4, 1913, Tuskegee, Alabama;
activist, organizer, recipient of the Congressional Gold Medal
of Honor in 1999, "Mother of the Civil Rights Movement"

When Rosa Parks refused to give up her seat to a white man on a segregated Alabama bus, she sparked a transit boycott that lasted three hundred and eighty-one days and made Montgomery the focal point of the national Civil Rights Movement. I was only eight years old, but the morning the bus company capitulated, my Alabama-born grandfather showed me the headline in delighted disbelief. "If it can happen in Alabama," he said, "it can happen anywhere."

LEONTYNE PRICE

Born February 10, 1927, Laurel, Mississippi;
singer, Metropolitan Opera leading lyric soprano,
Grammy Award winner, recipient of the Presidential
Medal of Freedom in 1964

When I was growing up on the west side of Detroit in the sixties, the music playing in most of the houses on our block was pure Motown. My mother didn't care. She was a fan of Leontyne Price, particularly as the doomed Cio-Cio-San in Puccini's opera *Madama Butterfly.* After a while, my friends got used to the strange music pouring unapologetically from my mother's upstairs window. Although I was a little embarrassed at the time, when I think about real love songs, Miss Price's rendition of "Un Bel Di" is still in my top five.

DELLA REESE
Born July 6, 1931, Detroit, Michigan;
singer, Emmy-nominated television and film actress, talk
show host, recipient of star on the Hollywood Walk of Fame

Della Reese is one of those people who makes everything she does look effortless. In 1969, when she became the first African American woman with her own prime-time talk and variety show, she opened the door that Oprah Winfrey would step through fifteen years later. *Touched by an Angel* was the name of her long-running television show, but it is also a phrase that could describe her life.

DIANA ROSS

Born March 26, 1944, Detroit, Michigan;
singer, Oscar-nominated film and television actress, author

Essence magazine, knowing my fear of flying, still asked me to go to Amsterdam to interview Diana Ross as she embarked on an international solo tour. I couldn't say no. The flight was uneventful, and she couldn't have been nicer. Arriving on time, she flipped back her famously extravagant hair, kicked off her five-inch heels, and curled up on the couch for a talk like we were girlfriends. The next night at the concert, when Miss Ross sang her hit song "Muscles," my normally undemonstrative husband leaped up from his second-row seat and flexed for all he was worth. When she pointed at him from the stage and smiled, I knew he could die a happy man.

Naomi Sims

Born March 30, 1949, Oxford, Mississippi;
fashion model, businesswoman, covers of Ladies' Home
Journal, New York Times Fashions of the Times,
Life Magazine, *and* Cosmopolitan

Breaking down barriers with her style, grace, and
brown-skinned beauty, Naomi Sims was the first
black model my generation knew by name—the
walking, talking embodiment of our slogan "Black is
beautiful!" Her picture was on our dorm room bul-
letin boards right beside pictures of radical activists
Angela Davis and Kathleen Cleaver. When she
smiled out at us from the cover of the *Ladies' Home
Journal,* we let the revolution rest for a minute and
smiled back.

TINA TURNER

Born November 26, 1939, Brownsville, Tennessee;
singer, author, inducted into the Rock and Roll
Hall of Fame in 1991

If we had seen the pain behind Tina Turner's power-house performances with the *Ike and Tina Turner Revue*, I like to believe we would have intervened, called for backup, and spirited our sister out of harm's way. But we didn't know, until she told us everything in her amazing memoir, *I, Tina,* and in songs like "What's Love Got To Do with It?" that said it all. These days, when Tina Turner takes your hands and smiles, there is no bitterness, no regret, no confusion. There is only peace that flows from her like its own kind of music.

CICELY TYSON

Born December 19, 1933, New York, New York;
model, stage actress, Oscar-nominated screen actress, Emmy
winner for The Autobiography of Miss Jane Pittman,
inducted into the Black Filmmakers Hall of Fame in 1977

There is a moment in Cicely Tyson's Oscar–nominated performance in the film *Sounder* when her character, Rebecca, glimpses her beloved husband coming home after months in jail, during which the family barely survived. She whispers his name over and over, afraid to believe it's really him, and then runs into his arms, weeping in relief and celebration. The scene is a powerful evocation of a love that endures, and of all her amazing stage and screen performances, that brief moment is the one that still moves me to tears.

Alice Walker

Born February 9, 1944, Eatonton, Georgia;
poet, novelist, activist, essayist, recipient of the Pulitzer Prize
for The Color Purple

Alice Walker is my personal *shero.* The fearlessness of her writing always moves and inspires me. As a young woman, having my first success as a writer, I was often terrified of the demands and responsibilities of this new life. Flying around the country, signing books, and sharing my work with new people at every stop, I sometimes found myself exhausted, overwhelmed, and weepy. At those moments, I'd ask myself one question: *What would Alice Walker do?* The answer was always the same: *Take a deep breath and get on with it.*

DIONNE WARWICK

Born December 12, 1940, East Orange, New Jersey;
singer, multiple Grammy Award winner,
television show host

Dionne Warwick's voice doesn't remind you of any-one else's. It is her own unique gift, creating an inti-mate exchange with her listeners that cannot be duplicated. I remember hearing her sing "Walk On By" when I was still in high school and running to the record store to buy the album. She looked so elegant in the cover photo, wearing a long white gown, more like a jazz singer than the Motown girls I was used to, but her voice defied categorization. It didn't matter what you called it. The important thing was, you couldn't resist it. I still can't.

NANCY WILSON
Born February 20, 1937, Chillicothe, Ohio;
singer, Emmy Award winner for The Nancy Wilson
Show, *multiple Grammy Award winner*

The first time I went to Jamaica as a summer ex-
change student at the University of Kingston, I dis-
covered that one of the boys in my literature class
was a fiend for Nancy Wilson. A group of us went
to his house one evening and had a great time lis-
tening to his cherished collection of her records.
Through the open windows, from the darkness of the
nearby Blue Mountains, we could hear the muffled
drums of a gathering of Rastafarians, while inside
my friend's house, Nancy Wilson was singing "How
Glad I Am." I'm sure Bob Marley would have ap-
proved.

Oprah Winfrey
Born January 29, 1954, Kosciusko, Mississippi;
talk show host, actress, producer, philanthropist,
world changer

Our hostess for the *Legends Weekend* wasn't sure she wanted to be included in the list of remarkable women whose names we were calling in our praise poem. We young 'uns argued that as the one whose vision had brought us all together she certainly belonged there. Feeling our oats, we also said we were prepared to overrule her objections and call her name anyhow. *I still am.*

ABOUT THE AUTHORS

PEARL CLEAGE is the author of four novels, including *Babylon Sisters* and *What Looks Like Crazy on an Ordinary Day . . .*, and a dozen plays, including *Flyin' West* and *Blues for an Alabama Sky*. Her new novel, *Baby Brother's Blues*, will be published by Ballantine/One World in the spring of 2006.

ZARON W. BURNETT, JR. is a novelist and theatre artist and the award-winning creator of the "Live at Club Zebra!" performance series. He is currently at work on the screen adaptation of his novel *The Carthaginian Honor Society*. Frequent collaborators, Pearl and Zaron make their home in southwest Atlanta.

ABOUT THE TYPE

The text of this book was set in Nofret, a typeface designed in 1986 by Gudrun Zapf-von Hesse especially for the Berthold foundry.